A ROOKIE BIOGRAPHY

HANS CHRISTIAN ANDERSEN

Prince of Storytellers

By Carol Greene

CHILDRENS PRESS®
CHICAGO

This book is for Raymond Kania.

Hans Christian Andersen (1805-1875)

Library of Congress Cataloging-in-Publication Data

Greene, Carol.
    Hans Christian Andersen : (prince of storytellers) / by Carol Greene.
        p.   cm. — (A Rookie biography)
    Includes index.
    Summary: A simple biography of the nineteenth-century Danish author
known for his fairy tales.
    ISBN 0-516-04219-X
    1. Andersen, H. C. (Hans Christian), 1805-1875—Biography—Juvenile
literature. 2. Authors, Danish—19th century—Biography—Juvenile
literature. [1. Andersen, H. C. (Hans Christian). 1805-1875. 2. Authors,
Danish.] I. Title. II. Series: Greene, Carol. Rookie biography.
PT8119.G67   1991
839.8′136—dc20
[92]
[B]   90-19903
                                                         CIP
                                                          AC

Hans Christian Andersen
was a real person.
He lived from 1805 to 1875.
He wrote many stories
about many things,
such as "The Little Mermaid"
and "The Ugly Duckling."
This is his own story.

TABLE OF CONTENTS

The city of Odense, Denmark (above), looked like this when Hans was a boy.
Hans's house (below) still stands in Odense. It is now a museum.

Chapter 1

Home

In a tiny house
in Odense, Denmark,
lived a boy named
Hans Christian Andersen.

His family was poor.
But Hans was happy
because his home was
full of love and stories.

Hans's father read to him.
His grandma told him tales,
and so did her friends.

Hans's father also made
a toy theater for him.
It had dolls for actors.
Hans used them
to act out stories.

Home was a happy place.
But school was not.
Other children
did not like Hans.

He looked strange—
tall and skinny,
with big hands, big feet,
and a big nose.

Hans was sad when the children made fun of him.

Sometimes Hans acted strange.
That was because he
wanted others to like him.
But Hans tried too hard.
The other children
made fun of him.

7

Then Hans would hurry
home to his family
and his stories.
Soon he felt happy again.

When Hans was 11,
his father died.
His mother had to work
to buy food.
She went out
to wash people's clothes.

Hans made up stories for the dolls
in his toy theater to act out.

Hans stayed home.
He began to make up
his own stories
for the doll actors
in his toy theater.

9

Then Hans's mother
got married again.
The family moved
to a house with
a garden by a river.

Hans loved to stand
in that garden and sing.
He made up a story
about a Chinese prince.

In the story Hans wrote,
the prince heard him sing,
took him to China, and
made him rich and famous.

Hans sang songs in this garden by the Odense River (above).
In Hans's story, a prince carried him away to China (below).

But that didn't happen.
Instead, Hans's mother said
he must soon get a job.
He could sew clothes.

Hans hated that idea.
He had a better one.
He would go to
the big city, Copenhagen,
and become an actor.

"I shall be famous,"
he said. "You first
go through an awful lot
of bad things, and
then you become famous."

And when Hans was 14,
off he went.

Tall ships from all over the world came to Copenhagen's busy port.

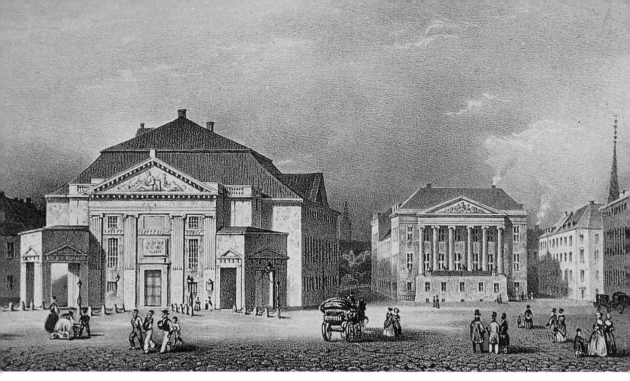

The Royal Theater in Copenhagen (above, at left). The houses in Copenhagen today (below) look much like they did in Hans Christian Andersen's time.

Chapter 2

A Job for Hans

Hans found a room
in big, busy Copenhagen.
Then he hurried
to the Royal Theater.

He talked to a dancer,
but she couldn't help him.
He talked to the director,
but he couldn't help either.

"Now what?" thought Hans.
He had almost no money.
Maybe he should try
the Royal Choir School.
After all, he could sing.

So Hans met Mr. Siboni,
head of the choir school.
He and his friends helped Hans.

Soon Hans was busy.
He did some singing.
He did some dancing.
He wrote some stories.

Hans made these paper cutouts when he was a boy in Odense.

Some days Hans had a job.
Some days he didn't.
He was often hungry.
But he prayed a lot,
and he kept on trying.

17

Christian VIII was the Danish king who helped Hans.

At last, someone talked
to the king about him.
The king said Hans
must go back to school.
He would pay Hans's fees.

The school was in
a town called Slagelse.
Hans was older than
the other boys.
But he didn't know as much.

The head of the school
made fun of him.
He called him "a stupid boy."
That hurt Hans.

The head also said Hans
must not write stories.
But Hans wrote them anyway.
Writing stories always
made him feel better.

At last, Hans went back
to study in Copenhagen.
He passed a big test
and wrote even more.

Today, schoolchildren
visit Hans Christian
Andersen's home and
look at the statue
of the beloved
storyteller.

He wrote a travel book
that people liked.
He wrote a play.
People liked the play too.
He wrote a book of poems.
People loved it.

Then Hans knew
what he was.
No more school for him.
He was a writer.

Chapter 3

The First Fairy Tales

Next, Hans took a trip
around Denmark.
He met a girl
and fell in love.
But she didn't love him.
Hans felt terrible.

Back in Copenhagen, a writer
made fun of Hans's writing.
Hans felt even worse.
Then his friends said
he didn't write well.
They said he should grow up.

Poor Hans was glad
when the king gave him
money for a long trip.
He went all over Europe.
He liked Italy best.

On his trip to Italy, Hans visited Rome.

Hans made these drawings of places
in Rome while he was visiting Italy.

When Hans got home,
he stopped listening
to his friends.
He just wrote the way
he wanted to write.

He wrote a book about Italy.
He wrote four fairy tales.
Then he wrote another book
and three more fairy tales.

23

A statue of Andersen's Little Mermaid (left) sits on a rock in the harbor of Copenhagen. The artist Vilhelm Pedersen drew this illustration of the Little Mermaid (right) for Hans's story.

At first, Hans said
the tales weren't important.
But he kept writing them.
He knew the tales
were important to him.

"'The Little Mermaid'
moved me deeply," he said.

Children knew the tales
were important, too.
They loved Hans
and gave him flowers.

Hans loved to read his fairy tales to young people.

Then older people
began to see that Hans
was a fine writer.
The government promised to
give him money each year
for the rest of his life.

Hans would never
be poor again.

Chapter 4

Prince Hans

Hans took more trips.
Everywhere he went,
he made new friends.
In Germany, he rode a train.
Trains were new then.
"You seem to fly!" said Hans.

The first trains looked like the one in this picture.
The smoke came from wood or coal burned as fuel.

Hans also went on
writing his fairy tales.
He had no trouble
finding ideas for them.
Hans saw stories everywhere.

He told a friend,
"Every little flower says,
'Just look at me.
Then you'll know my story.'"

Once Hans saw a picture
of a poor girl selling matches.
That gave him the idea
for "The Little Match Girl."

The Little Match Girl

Once a little boy
gave him a tin soldier
to keep him company.
Hans put the boy and
the soldier in "The Old House."

An artist drew
this illustration
for Hans's story
"The Steadfast
Tin Soldier."

One day, Hans felt sad.
He went for a walk
in the woods and fields.
There he had an idea
for another story.

At first, Hans called it
"The Story of a Duck."
But it ended up as
"The Ugly Duckling."
Hans put his feelings
in his stories, too.

In Andersen's story "The Emperor's New Clothes," one little boy has the courage to point out that the "new clothes" the emperor is wearing are no clothes at all.

"I believe," he said, "that the best thing I can do is to write these tales."

Hans still had bad times. Some of his friends died. He fell in love with a singer, Jenny Lind. She didn't love him.

Hans Christian Andersen (left)
fell in love with Jenny Lind (below),
a Swedish singer.

But the tales always
helped Hans feel better.

One day, he met
a little princess.
She said Hans
was a prince, too.
He was the Prince of Storytellers.

This statue of Hans Christian Andersen is in the town hall square in Copenhagen.

Chapter 5

The Swan

As Hans grew older,
he had more good times.
Old friends died,
but he made new ones,
and he still loved trips.

One day, he took
a very special trip
back to his hometown, Odense.
Children left school
to welcome Hans,
and a band played.

At City Hall, the mayor
made a speech about him.
There was a big dinner,
singing, and dancing.

After dark, people marched
through town with torches.
A light was put
in every window of
every house.
"We are proud of you, Hans,"
those lights seemed to say.

The people of Odense honored Hans with a torchlight parade.

Hans sits on the step of a coach that belonged to his
friends the Melchiors (left). It was at their country home
that Hans died peacefully in his sleep.

Hans said that day was
the finest day in his life.

When he was 67,
Hans became sick.
He never really got well.
At last, some friends
took him to their home
in the country.

Villa Rolighed, the house where Hans Christian Andersen died

There Hans dreamed
in the beautiful garden
or rested in bed.
He felt happy
and full of peace.

Hans Christian Andersen
died very quietly
on August 4, 1875,
and all the bells
in Copenhagen rang.

Throughout his life, Hans made
fancy paper cutouts (left)
and wrote stories.

Years before, a boy named
Pen Browning said that
Hans might look like
an ugly duckling.
But his mind had
become a beautiful swan.

Today, children everywhere
know that Pen Browning was right.
They still love Hans Christian Andersen,
the Prince of Storytellers.

Important Dates

1805   April 2—Born at Odense, Denmark, to Hans and Anne-Marie Andersen

1819   Left home for Copenhagen

1822   Began school in Slagelse

1835   Wrote first fairy tales

1838   Given yearly pension from government

1840   Rode on a train

1867   Became honorary citizen of Odense

1875   August 4—Died at Rolighed, Denmark

INDEX

Page numbers in boldface type indicate illustrations.

PHOTO CREDITS

ABOUT THE AUTHOR

Carol Greene has degrees in English literature and musicology. She has worked in international exchange programs, as an editor, and as a teacher. She now lives in St. Louis, Missouri, and writes full-time. She has published more than eighty books. Others in the Rookie Biographies series include *Ludwig van Beethoven, Black Elk, Elizabeth Blackwell, Daniel Boone, Christopher Columbus, Jacques Cousteau, Elizabeth the First, Benjamin Franklin, Martin Luther King, Jr., Robert E. Lee, Abraham Lincoln, John Muir, Louis Pasteur, Pocahontas, Jackie Robinson, George Washington,* and *Laura Ingalls Wilder.*